WHAT IS CODING?

Steffi Cavell-Clarke & Thomas Welch

COMPUTERS AND <CODING>

KidHaven PUBLISHING

Published in 2019 by KidHaven Publishing, an Imprint of Greenhaven Publishing, LLC
353 3rd Avenue, Suite 255, New York, NY 10010

Written by: Steffi Cavell-Clarke & Thomas Welch
Edited by: Kirsty Holmes
Designed by: Danielle Jones

Cataloging-in-Publication Data

Names: Cavell-Clarke, Steffi. | Welch, Thomas.
Title: What is coding? / Steffi Cavell-Clarke & Thomas Welch.
Description: New York : KidHaven Publishing, 2019. | Series: Computers and coding | Includes glossary and index.
Identifiers: ISBN 9781534527041 (pbk.) | ISBN 9781534527034 (library bound) | ISBN 9781534527058 (6 pack)
Subjects: LCSH: Coding theory--Juvenile literature. | Computer programming--Juvenile literature.
Classification: LCC QA268.C38 2019 | DDC 005.13'3--dc23

IMAGE CREDITS

Cover – izabel.l, 1000s_pixels, Macrovector, danjazzia. 5 – Inspiring. 6 – Born_Rich_japan. 7 – Teguh Jati Prasetyo, Bloomicon. 8–9 – Pogorelova Olga, Maksim M, 32 pixels, Dacian G. 10 – Jane Kelly, venimo. 11 – 1000s_pixels. 12 – LITUSPRO, Jane Kelly. 14 – Kit8.net, Sudowoodo. 15 – Succo Design. 16 – MikeStyle, Sudowoodo. 18–20 – Scratch is developed by the Lifelong Kindergarten Group at the MIT Media Lab. See http://scratch.mit.edu".
22 – venimo, venimo. 23 – Abscent.

Printed in the United States of America

CPSIA compliance information: Batch #BS18KL: For further information contact Greenhaven Publishing LLC, New York, New York at 1-844-317-7404.

WHAT IS CODING?

COMPUTERS AND <CODING>

Words that look like **this** can be found in the glossary on page 24.

WHAT IS A COMPUTER?

A computer is a **machine** that can be taught to do something by itself. Computers do not have brains like us. They cannot think or have ideas, but they can follow **instructions** and do lots of useful things.

DID YOU KNOW?

There are over 1 billion computers around the world.

A computer is made up of lots of different parts that have their own **functions**.

Camera

Screen

Mouse

USB Stick

Power Button

Keyboard

Trackpad

Compact Disc

WHAT IS CODE?

Code is a way of giving instructions to a computer. There are lots of different ways to code, but they all do the same thing – tell a computer what to do, and in what order.

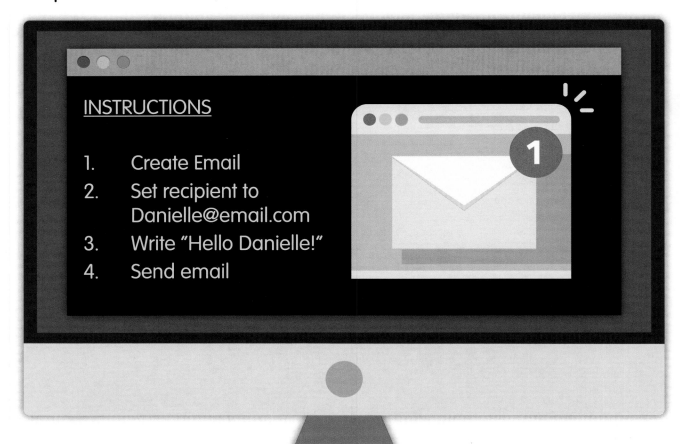

INSTRUCTIONS

1. Create Email
2. Set recipient to Danielle@email.com
3. Write "Hello Danielle!"
4. Send email

Code is very useful. Once a person has given instructions to a computer in code, the computer can follow the instructions on its own.

WHAT IS AN ALGORITHM?

Algorithms are like strings of instructions that tell computers how to do things.

1.

Open the toothpaste.

2.

Put a bit of toothpaste on the toothbrush.

3.

Open your mouth.

If you were a computer, this would be the algorithm for brushing your teeth:

Each step in an algorithm needs to be really simple and **precise**. Computers can't think for themselves or guess, so we need to tell them exactly what to do.

4.

Brush your teeth for two minutes.

5.

Rinse your mouth with water.

6. Smile!

Algorithms are written and given to a computer in a language it understands. These written algorithms are called code.

WHAT IS A PROGRAM?

A collection of algorithms, written in code, is called a program. Programs can do many things, such as telling time, reminding you when your homework is due, or playing a game. You can write programs for almost anything.

However, sometimes programs don't work in the way the **coder** expects them to. You should always check that your programs are working properly. A mistake in code is called a bug.

COMPUTER
LANGUAGES

There are lots of different coding languages – Java, C#, Python, Haskell, Lisp, Ruby, HTML, XML, CSS, and many more.

Different languages can make it easier to do different things. HTML is great for creating a **webpage**, but Java or Swift might be better for creating **mobile apps**.

This is because some of the languages, like HTML, are **designed** to be good at showing information on a screen, while others, like Python, are designed to be good at deciding what to do with that information.

HTML

PYTHON

WHY DO WE NEED PROGRAMS?

Simple algorithms are fine if we just want a computer to do one thing. But if we want a computer to do more things, we need more than one algorithm. Like a recipe for a meal might include lots of things, a program contains lots of algorithms.

CODING RECIPE BOOK

Programs can help computers do complicated things. A smartphone can play a game, store information, make a phone call, send a text message, and access the Internet – all at once! It needs a lot of algorithms to do that. Programs keep the algorithms organized so they can work better.

HISTORY OF CODE

The first computers only did math. They were HUGE machines that filled whole rooms and were slow – nothing like the computers we have today! Back then, even a simple algorithm could take days to compute.

Ada Lovelace

Ada Lovelace was the first person to write computer programs, in the 1800s! She predicted that one day computers would do more than just math.

Charles Babbage

Charles Babbage designed a machine called the Analytical Engine in the 1800s. It would have been the first modern computer, but it was never built.

Alan Turing

Alan Turing created special computers in World War II that helped break codes. He is known as "The Father of Computer Science."

SCRATCH

Scratch is a language that has been designed to be easy for people to learn. Instead of having to write out code, it uses pictures to show how the program works. Users can move and change those pictures to change how the program works.

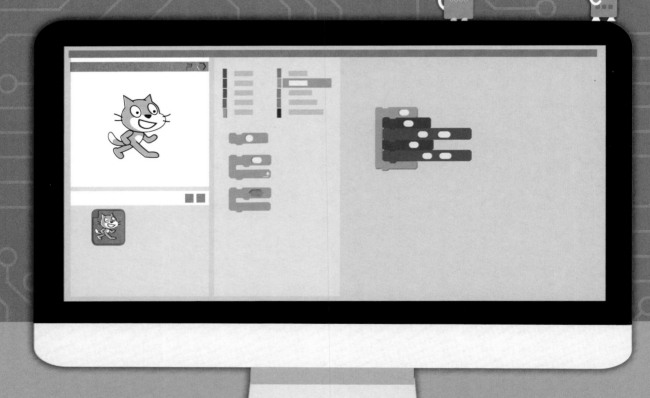

Here, a Scratch program makes the picture of a cat say "Hello!"

A SCRATCH PROGRAM

Scratch lets you create programs using pictures. This example shows how you can move a picture of a cat and make it ask what it should do next.

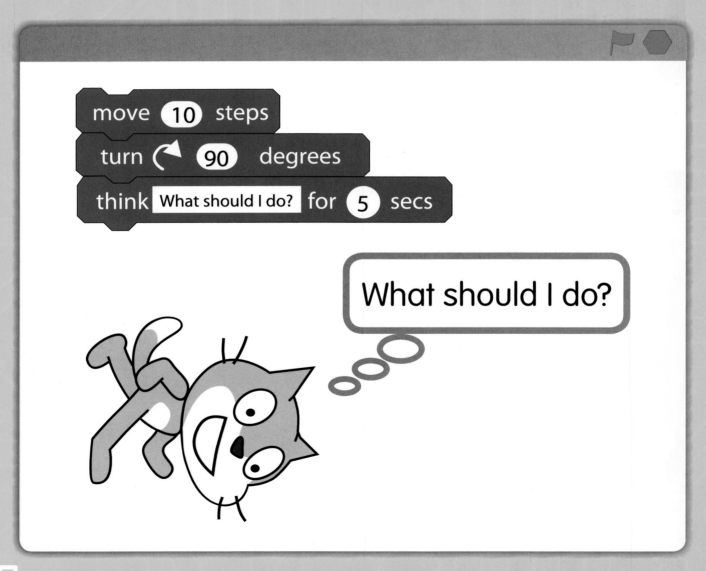

The algorithm the program follows is:

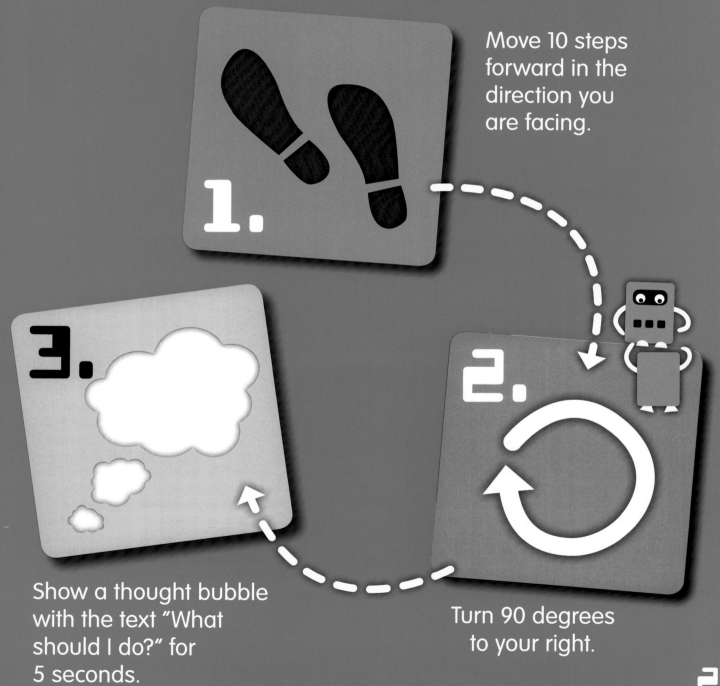

Move 10 steps forward in the direction you are facing.

1.

3.

2.

Show a thought bubble with the text "What should I do?" for 5 seconds.

Turn 90 degrees to your right.

DEBUGGING
A PROGRAM

It is common to find out that the code you have written doesn't do quite what you wanted it to. "Debugging" code can help you figure out what has gone wrong.

There are different ways to debug a program:
- carefully reading the code to make sure it is right
- printing out what the program is doing line by line
- stepping through it using a special debugging program

All these methods rely on thinking **logically** about what the program is doing and how it works.

GLOSSARY

CODER	someone who writes code
DESIGNED	planned for a specific purpose
FUNCTIONS	specific purposes or tasks
INSTRUCTIONS	detailed information explaining how something should be done
LOGICALLY	using careful thought and reasoning
MACHINE	a tool or device that performs a task
MOBILE APPS	programs that work on a mobile device, such as a smartphone
PRECISE	specific or accurate
WEBPAGE	pages of information on the Internet

INDEX